YOUNG SANTA

for Indigo

Copyright © 2025 by Joe Deany-Braun
All rights reserved.

Young Santa
ISBN 978-0-9967933-1-5

Library of Congress Control Number: 2025933341

Published by Thiessen Press
Fort Collins, CO

CONTENTS

Santa holds your invisible hand	1
Santa tells it like it is	2
Santa has some questions	3
Santa stares at the moon for too long	5
Santa comes down with cabin fever	6
Santa tries to distinguish between love and hunger	7
Intimations of the Naughty List	8
Canticle of the Reindeer	9
Santa takes a hike	15
Santa almost dies of exposure	16
Santa learns how to fly	17
Santa bathes in cold waters	19
Santa considers the fjord in relation to free will	20
Santa devises a semiotics of deep image	22
Santa dreams of a better world	23
Santa loses his faith in metaphor	24
Santa wonders if there is a God	25
Santa learns how to play the piano	26
Santa paraphrases Kepler's *Harmonices Mundi*	27
Santa follows the second star to the right	28
Santa's theory of metamorphosis	29
Santa tries to understand negative capability	32
Santa rages at the dying of the light	33
Santa works on his motorcycle	35
Otis teaches Santa how to catch gods	36

Santa abandons his plans to build an Ark	38
Santa does not know what he does not know	39
Santa reveals the essential nature of hope	49
Santa holds a grudge	50
Santa hallucinates the end of the Holocene	51
Santa can't remember how long he has been alive	52
The Gospel according to Santa	54
Santa loses his innocence	55
Santa tells you his biggest secret	56
Santa writes a prescription	57
Santa is deserted by poetry in his time of greatest need	58
Santa declutters the cosmological constant	59
Santa demystifies communion	60
Santa could have been a topologist	61
Santa learns to love his neighbor	62
Santa contemplates the meaning of motherhood	63
Santa tries to be a gracious host	65
Santa grows aware of the space behind him	67
The transmigration of Santa's soul	69
Not Santa's first rodeo	70
Santa searches for the beginning of time	71
Santa hears the voice of God	77

O God, give me words to make my dream-children live.

JOSEPH SEAMON COTTER, JR.

I am trying to steer the ship towards Christmas.

VAUGHN'S NEPHEW

SANTA HOLDS YOUR INVISIBLE HAND

We descend from
the pine-stippled shade into
a wide yellow

crock of hoary
light. Gold is the grasses'
million-headed dream.

You fill me
so full of the unseen
that I grieve.

Heaven is brown
for seed-feet like these.
Who if not

the dark land
sleeps our little bodies like
rain coming down?

SANTA TELLS IT LIKE IT IS

The whole world
reclines. The sun vomits light.
The trees explode.

SANTA HAS SOME QUESTIONS

Do you ever
think maybe we are supposed
to be smaller?

Do you think
that whatever your body knows
you also know?

Where is behind
a tree? Why does poison
make us happy?

What is a
thing if not edging always
into another thing?

Remember when the
moon was right over the
mountains all day?

With my hands
I am holding wait what
am I holding?

I wonder what
the smell of you and
me would be—

SANTA STARES AT THE MOON
FOR TOO LONG

We say reflection
we mean light interrupted light
beyond our bodies.

A strange light
it is and a strange
light to carry.

SANTA COMES DOWN WITH CABIN FEVER

> The sky salts
> our hut with shards of
> greyblue sea. We
>
> limesoft in the
> cool bower of pine trees
> ravaged by beetles.
>
> God there is
> no need for all this.
> God there is.

SANTA TRIES TO DISTINGUISH
BETWEEN LOVE AND HUNGER

In your hunger
is a large look that
like the sun

ripens and like
a plum is soft. I
spend all day

trying to feed
the lion but it only
wants to play.

Do you see
what the look in your
longing hunger lives

for? Did you
know that need is love
in the wild?

INTIMATIONS OF THE NAUGHTY LIST

There are men
like Humboldt who know thickets
stem by stem—

leaf by smiling
edge of teeth and moth
by startled wing

of eyes. There
are such men who find
their way by

feeding age its
fund of acts—such gushing
men who rise.

Men—such men
who tighten ties—hear nothing
but their cries.

CANTICLE OF THE REINDEER

> Inside I stand at the window, god,
> with your name wrapped round my throat
>   like a scarf
>
>   *Annie Dillard*

there's something tied
around yr neck and it
won't come off

*

if god then
fierce and total like the
gnash of teeth

not the moon
that broken light that o-
shun softened bone

*

you had been
running—the grasses lift and
pall and feld

your foot was
knowing—a quake in the
wide yellow tarn

*

this god how
taught in coil—no sound
to set free

*

you remember running
the knot of yr heart
of a net

knotted w others—
offer and clench offer and
clench—the drums

of yr feet
of yr feet in the
field—snowpack and

grass clay pock
pebbled loam—wheat sand soot
sun sun holy

*

open field of
the moon or open moon
of the field

i miss you
i know you—hairy star
fur breathing seed

*

so you have
known joy—you know how
it slips away

from the den
at night the self un-
seen for dark

like a tail
in tow—perhaps you have
known joy only

in the stake
sharp relief of its nose
against the sky

no hunger fit
to fold in a hand
but for sin

*

i saw people
in the shallow valley people
w legs like

the grasses and
ears for darkly brimful nights
we shared spheres

and a bowl
sloped w frozen pine and
the day turned

slow and tied
watery bows in and around
and through and

through us the
wind a whiskered thing nudged
us and knew

*

my impulse is
racing over far tracts roughed
out for quarry

when our dark
dozens gathered, joined by the
night falling in

*

all farther who
art in heather fallow be
thy range thy

winged run thy
hill become in earth what
claw do leaven

give us this
clay our gait and tread
and lift us

thru passes and
ridge buckld grasses to steer
away from starvation

feed us not
unto tameness for whine is
the signal pitch

pine the bower
hoarfrost gunpowder git heel the
story all when

*

what crosses are
those they carry thru the
quiet slanting light

what dust so
wet for skin what soft
and swollen hearts

*

baffled and aching
i stand on two legs
able to bow

SANTA TAKES A HIKE

In search of
angels we roam the hazel
hide of dusk.

No numbers suck
the marrow of this bone-
less almost being.

SANTA ALMOST DIES OF EXPOSURE

A stone will
sit in a field for
an aeon while

the wave-ends
crash their days against the
days. Thousands and

thousands of bones
away the wonder-bird wheels
like fire on

a string. Who
is the wonder-bird? Who
is the string?

SANTA LEARNS HOW TO FLY

The wind came
over and over the water
and the rock

and the tree
rattled and the trees rattled
in shocked spots

on the hill
and the tree was one
tree and one

tree was one
tree and the one tree
was one singing

cone of swung
green and cones of ink
on the hill

and the hill
and hill that are hills
and dusk and

water as wings
endless wings who fold all
space in two

SANTA BATHES IN COLD WATERS

    to that blue that
    curls around the crumbling, to that

    Jack Collom

of the not-
yet night, in love with
skin whose bone

in loving curls
with clay, the thought of
almost coming day

the dream to
be the one who wakes
the dream who

wakes the bone
by lung, and someone says
goodbye cold love

and love almost
becoming clay whose bone is
not yet night

begins to dream
and in the dream to
pray, and in

the inner dream
to drown, and then to
wake, and moan.

SANTA CONSIDERS THE FJORD
IN RELATION TO FREE WILL

The quick no-
thing of your simple yes-
ing heart goes

like a cliff-
broken rock down down for
some big water.

SANTA DEVISES A SEMIOTICS OF DEEP IMAGE

A tree, collaps'd
into another's arms: a person—
you or me—

so tired, may-
be grieving. A giant rock
shoulder giving pause

then the plunge
into shadow, my little heart
full of heat.

A sudden thicket
of knee deep aspen. (They
share something like

words underground.) Skin-
soft bark scarred with initials.
A brown move-

ment, no guile.
Two eyes, four—the warm
glow of sentience.

SANTA DREAMS OF A BETTER WORLD

If only "white"
was "snow" and not the
other way around.

SANTA LOSES HIS FAITH IN METAPHOR

A nun walks
with two dogs through the
late morning light

in the wind;
the heavy bells are silent
as the sun

strikes the belfry.
Earth moans in the silence
of bell-shaped

light—moans a
koan that words can only
dream of shelt'ring.

SANTA WONDERS IF THERE IS A GOD

For every wing
a claw; the beak and
jaw just hinges.

Brittle thing, mid-
song, clings; yawning sod of
cold wet hunger.

Where to go
from here? The small heart
robed in shudders.

Somewhere warm and
still. Still. From awful thrill
to such dumb

hands, paper towel
and grocery bag. Somewhere dark
and still. Still.

SANTA LEARNS HOW TO PLAY THE PIANO

Muscle memory is
the smallest bird your broken
hands can hold.

The least you
can do is also perhaps
the very best.

SANTA PARAPHRASES KEPLER'S
HARMONICES MUNDI

The ridge was
swallowing the sun, and I
could hear wings

that I could
not hear. Something dragged out
of the garden

by the cat,
still-closed eyes but alive
and—and shivering.

Not long now,
not long. There must always
be the moon—

the remembrance, the
relief. The blinds raised. The
door flung open.

SANTA FOLLOWS THE SECOND STAR
TO THE RIGHT

There was no
one. The sun fell out
of its peel

in the sky
and the yellow of bells
could be heard

for an age.
There was no one and
then there was

you. No—night
with elbow scars all bright
in the heart

and crab apple
knees; with skin, without sight.
And then? You:

the dell behind
space: the hollowed-out dream
of your face.

SANTA'S THEORY OF METAMORPHOSIS

We are in
a small room and you
are looking at

me and I
am looking at you and
there is nothing

to say and
nothing happens except you blink
and all the

lights in the
world go out the spider
silk between your

kneecaps snaps with
a sound like the end
of a prayer

the roaring naked
heart of silence grinds and
widens you pull

a thread of
air through the simple closed
curve of your

body grieving where
cleft raw where turned from
cool and few

to sundry a
secret muscle-bound edict ritual
drunk on color

you swim thread-
less wanting nothing bare as
snow wet as

driftwood near to
gnosis a tidal coolth of
shadow setting through

the ridge like
sleep you swim that earth
would let such

slip such clots
of ocean roll and sweep
such snowdry sun

the naked trees
and doors you swim you
swim to me

SANTA TRIES TO UNDERSTAND
NEGATIVE CAPABILITY

Everything belongs in
the book that will never
be written: the

low blue winter
clouds in the dying day
belong, as do

the black limbs
that clutch at space and
make love. And

what of us—
do we belong in the
book of blue

clouds dying days
winter limbs and loving space?
I want to

say yes. But
someone has to not write
the never book.

SANTA RAGES AT THE DYING
OF THE LIGHT

Every fifty yards
or so, you look up
from the footworn

furrows of dirt
as if called. Here am
I. Fifty paces—

transorbital lunge, allure
of flung space lit from
below. The one

light has fallen.
You are made large by
the longing, for

it. Primate, alone
in an antediluvian bed of
rabbitbrush and flax.

The flats are
not without their folds. Your
lungs hold some

air and offer.
Earth heaves, light cleaves. It
is almost enough.

SANTA WORKS ON HIS MOTORCYCLE

Every part touches
another part part of a
whole in touch

made whole by
witness holy delusion of the
double and one.

OTIS TEACHES SANTA HOW TO CATCH GODS

I saw him
on my way down from
the deeping gulch

in the lemony
fields of folded light, blue
grama and rabbitbrush.

Otis, what are
you doing here? I asked.
Well, he said

Seeing as the
sun is going down, I
figured the moon

would be coming
up, and in that dark
sort of glow

there's always at
least one god sniffing around
in the underbrush

and such, and
so I come to watch
for the gods

and listen to
their soft noises and think
on their meanings.

Otis, I said,
I was just doing the
very same thing.

SANTA ABANDONS HIS PLANS
TO BUILD AN ARK

If my body
was a giant hand, I'd
run my palm

over the fibrous
hide of the foothills and
call it deer;

with my fingers
I'd comb the pines and
call it cat.

As it is
my body is small and
I have no

real calling, except
what shakes in the shell
of my chest.

SANTA DOES NOT KNOW WHAT HE DOES NOT KNOW

> Entire body looks for nothing.
> Living, I plunge into Yellow Springs.
> *Dogen*

Where the fire
is far and blue, and
blue and many.

*

Every song is
the song of my family
trying to live.

*

Some old country
some far brown proud tree
makes me lonely.

*

So precious to
spend even three minutes with
a strange warmth.

*

To be known
press here; to be un-
known, press here.

*

There is nothing
like the slow blue evening
in this poem.

*

If I could
show you the blue, it
would not count.

*

How far the
blue hill, how much more
than some light.

*

The stars in
the snow are so numerous.
Something's going on.

*

Big dogs herd
the wet-nosed cows, their
paw-soft eyes.

*

So little need
be said, yet we say
all we can.

*

A deep bodily
listening and the smell of
grass at night.

*

Green stains and
big holes where light is
a howling dog.

*

Fed and full
of knots upon the tongue
in throat swallow.

*

When it goes
it comes it depends it
will find you.

*

God we have
some difficult questions difficult like
watching the wind.

*

I find blueberries
in the best poems. They
taste like blueberries.

*

These days are
too much sometimes they are
just too much.

*

The unseeable animal
is preposterous, and so is
the loving darkness.

*

The limitless blue
is so bright because of
all that churning.

*

The blue sky
baffling us all before we
even eat breakfast.

*

An old rusted
moth swinging around the bulb
delirious and certain.

*

A day sufficiently
slow in the body, and
suddenly the sky.

*

The squirrel shakes
rain from its birthday brown
soft and quick.

*

A weed blooms
orange. Breezy purple iris flag.
Eyes boom black.

*

Snow falls overnight.
Heavy leaves and wet light.
Green and white.

*

Wet grass blue
and slow in the heavy
light of morning.

*

The doorknob hovers
at waist height, wringing itself
like a bloom.

*

The rich ground
heaves. The sky dryly weeps.
The circle circles.

*

I am melting
from laughter and your hands
in my jacket.

*

Between the two
of us is a valley
and a river.

*

I love you
like the piano is not
black and white.

*

When you go
no let's no no forget
let's the cold.

*

If you would
yes let's yes yes let's
until it goes.

*

The only words
in the whole world are
"one more time."

*

Lungs are big
floppy ears on either side
of the heart.

*

When I dream
of dying, I wake up
as red wine.

*

We wake wet
with chain link legs with
legs like melody.

*

The skin of
a moment, breathing like a
river, the lips.

*

There is not
enough of more for everybody
to get some.

*

Dark blue flower.
And the wishes and the
wants all simper.

*

The voice as
an autumn leaf in the
wind of spring.

*

The cellar door
in shadow and the ground
in broken light.

*

Someday we will
go home I think but
maybe home goes.

*

There will be
songs—we will sing them
in the dark.

SANTA REVEALS THE ESSENTIAL
NATURE OF HOPE

How does it
happen, the stones on the
hillside, the river-

broken sweep of
steep earth and my body
watching it run?

Nothing better for
the soul than utter ruin,
which summons hope

like a pollen
shattered on the little wind
of Big Time.

SANTA HOLDS A GRUDGE

Looks like a
pine cone, feels like a
snowball, sounds like

a fipple flute,
smells like a hedgehog. Well
now you know.

SANTA HALLUCINATES THE END
OF THE HOLOCENE

In the night
a small slope of green
forms under my

dream head like
a field of grain folding
slow in summer

wind. Who lives
there in the knoll of
night? River of

ice long since
drawn up to the sun
in this heat

give us trees
give us something to name.
I hear bone-

flutes down by
the straw. I am going
to say goodbye.

SANTA CAN'T REMEMBER HOW LONG HE HAS BEEN ALIVE

The sun does
not come upon the meadow
all at once.

First, birds that
you cannot see. The thought
of light far

beyond the trees
and warmth is a promise
you won't believe.

Knees, chief among
the sundry knuckles of your
body, like rocks.

Then a breeze,
some long ago prayer whispered
in ecstasy, and

you feel day's
desire to exist. The sun
does not come

upon the meadow
all at once. The meadow
wakes up slow.

THE GOSPEL ACCORDING TO SANTA

A human is
born who will surely die.
God help us.

SANTA LOSES HIS INNOCENCE

In the garden
in my dream all the
fruit was ripe.

We were shadows
in a pleasure thick air
of dark trees.

You had creek-
bed cheeks I was too
afraid to eat.

The sun hung
there below the belt like
a bell and

the color was
a season and the sound
was a spell.

SANTA TELLS YOU HIS BIGGEST SECRET

Every eleven years
the sun's magnetic field flips.
Eleven-year cycles

have been found
in tree-ring thicknesses and
hundred-million-year-

old lake-bottom
layers of siltstone. There are
eleven thumb keys

on a bassoon,
not counting the whisper key.
There are eleven

spacetime dimensions in
M-theory. There are eleven
rules for catching

gods. Number one:
Open your hands. Number two:
Close your eyes.

SANTA WRITES A PRESCRIPTION

Ride a motorcycle.
Chase something. Lose your hat
in the wind.

Look hard at
a faraway tree. Walk in
the dark. Read

a language you
don't speak. Stop making promises.
Renounce the idea

of yourself. Rename
the savior. Press the off
button. Hold still.

SANTA IS DESERTED BY POETRY
IN HIS GREATEST TIME OF NEED

Our lives pass
in holy phantasm of personhood
split like wood.

In eulogy, there
is room made for all
the love a

person cannot bear.
You hold me now as
I held him

who is you.
This is *La Pietà* in
miniature, the manifold

of virtue like
a shroud over skin: we
know the shape

of love even
as it slips our grasp.
We hang on.

SANTA DECLUTTERS THE COSMOLOGICAL CONSTANT

Contractions are instinctual
in birth and in speech.
A dying boy

might have contractions
of the spirit and write
like fire. Some

ghost pulling his
body back into the womb.
No, you say

not possible.
Yes, I say, from the
bottom of my

bedroom, where the
ceiling confuses me for fruit
before the fall.

SANTA DEMYSTIFIES COMMUNION

Take and eat.
If you are not hungry,
do not eat.

SANTA COULD HAVE BEEN A TOPOLOGIST

Time, gesturing in
opposite directions with equal verve,
baffles the physics

of our most
evident truths. Speech is a
precious tone the

glacial heart hammers
into being. What is that
you hear now?

It must be
the cymbal of your snow-
capped starry mind.

SANTA LEARNS TO LOVE HIS NEIGHBOR

There's a dog
in that woman's bicycle basket.
She rides down

the September street.
There are voices all over—
they are soft

like stars in
the night. Where else would
stars be? In

the grass in
the morning—before time hits
the sun like

a baseball and
the ridge catches it like
an old glove.

SANTA CONTEMPLATES THE MEANING OF MOTHERHOOD

Do you think
the moon is not what
the moon hears

or is fearing
in the black black ever-
much of never

landing light? Do
you know what fearing looms
in daysome red

to fold plum
and stomach with no one
to hold near

and give grief?
The patterns pulse where we
would or would

not press down
and drown in. The end
is a swallow

in the buggy
dusk of streetlight crosshairs O
hold me now

dear song tell
ma I won't be long
O tell her.

SANTA TRIES TO BE A GRACIOUS HOST

Big thoughts visit
me like foreign dignitaries at
an all-night

diner. They spend
restless nights on the fleabitten
beds of my

cheap-hostel brain
and leave in the morning
after eating their

granola. I fry
eggs and clean their rooms—
I give them

everything I have.
If only they knew how
much it costs

to keep the
lights on. But they come
from lands where

light shines without
end. When they leave, we
take photos, shake

hands. I put
the photos in frames on
the walls where

other guests cannot
fail to notice them. "How
cool," they say,

"this place is
cool." "Yes," I say, "this
place is cool."

SANTA GROWS AWARE OF
THE SPACE BEHIND HIM

My sisters live
in the hills. I walk
miles and miles

through tall grasses
to see them. Day dies
while I walk

and the crucified
grasses glow, and the dome
of blue goes

electric with grief.
My sisters give me time
to get right.

Mostly my sisters
are secrets in shade. They
sleep where I

cannot imagine to
say. But soft like a
song in the

dun of done
day—grasses that reach, and
grasses that sway.

THE TRANSMIGRATION OF SANTA'S SOUL

I don't want
to die before seeing grass
in the wind

trees at night
tracks in the snow a
bird's eye closed.

I don't want
to leave this place but
I am hungry.

NOT SANTA'S FIRST RODEO

The gaze unimpeded
by the self in a
body would rush

around the world
like a lasso. I have
come in this

crisp nightblue dusk
to believe that someone is
holding the rope.

SANTA SEARCHES FOR
THE BEGINNING OF TIME

> How can one tell the difference between
> an image and an act of the will?
>
> *Antoine de Saint-Exupéry*

Ten thousand flowers
rustle on a dark plain—
the unspoken sun

a silent glow
behind the mountain. Soft wild
grass and heavy

light, a color
wan, howling. The field speaks
mostly cloven hooves

and punctate eyes
in the wordless stems—and
eyes like berries

darkly see the
rabbits catch their grassless eyes
in holy footflat

mud and light.
The brooding fist a golden
clutch of dreamings

golden wordless veins
and clustered stems that end
in gold—in

fist of dream
that clutch of eggs with
golden brooding wordless

light. Dry ground
holy star bitten gorse, wering
fringe of speckled

fawn, shootstill feld
limbs tender end, and so
many wings in

the wingless wind—
and so many wings in
the wingless wind.

*

We are on
the hilltop—a flood of
stars but still.

The fell day
blooms heedless on the rim
far snow along

the shale, where
glim wishes roam in crow
black night, magpie

sleights on slopes
of marl, cricket stirrups droll
collé, bodies my

one body hears
are knowing. The bending knees
of sightless grass

maundy lightspun petals
rare—so low so near
to dayclapped dusk.

The hill careening
wetlaced arch, void of wheels
yet heeling fire.

Old climb dipping
windless lap, moth dark hovel
hum dark mother.

Thought swollen hummock
drum in the reed, headless
cattails fractal seed.

*

The shower howls
in minutes child, nose against
her nettle breath.

You were summat
spelled in the lime—legless
shiver, tessellated rime.

Bitumen grail of
pleistocene dread, burlesque word in
a shrubbery hush.

Bear flute tooth
marks fingering the flues, chirp-
ridden sward of

long fallen sea—
throated ear of the wet
hour's moon, ringing

like hell in
the unhearing lug this making
might be madness.

*

In darkness holy
gravid blur, cardinal scrum of
mammal soft yarn

gut dark night
gasps as it spins—a
rushing sum, thing

herd overhead. Welkin
rockpool calm yet trembles. The
crackle of hatching

the shell under
sound, antediluvian plainsong sand, the
silence of abundant

shine, cold wet
stars and holy curves, auld
wain sign of

orb in eye—
slow umbrellas gown of hoar
whose heart belongs

beyond what breaks
now sets a hawk run
look run run.

*

We the reaching
vessels vassals, recipes eternal give.
Seafloor swell of

desert heave, part
lips to beg the gloam
for breath, for

lung red hunger
sprinting veins. Is heart not
growing still when

stopped? The deeping
well of treesleep hearing hollers
hidden groves be-

moan. Our lights
do not distract the sky.
The call cuts

through the bone
we carry home there is
no other way.

SANTA HEARS THE VOICE OF GOD

NOTES

"Intimations of the Naughty List" is after Andrea Wulf. The italicized stanzas in "Canticle of the Reindeer" are lineated excerpts from "Brought up by Wolves" by Diana Witherby (*Collected Poems*, 1973). "Santa bathes in cold waters" first appeared in *The Imaginable* (2024). "Santa learns how to fly" is for Alan Mudd. "Santa loses his faith in metaphor" is for David Mutschlecner. "Santa almost dies of exposure" is for Cookie Egret. "Otis teaches Santa how to catch gods" is for Todd Simmons. "Santa abandons his plans to build an Ark" is for Jeff Chelf.

"Santa does not know what he does not know" is for Elizabeth Fuller. "Santa reveals the essential nature of hope" appears in *A Poetic Inventory of the Cache la Poudre River* (2025). "Santa holds a grudge" is for Will Pass. "Santa is deserted by poetry in his greatest time of need" is for Auburn Wilson IV. "Santa declutters the cosmological constant" is after Max Ritvo. "Santa demystifies communion" is for Reed Bye. "Santa learns to love his neighbor" is after Natalie Bergman. "Santa tries to be a gracious host" is after Mark Leidner. "Santa searches for the beginning of time" is for Duna Reed.

The poems of *Young Santa* are made up of sequential lunes, or eleven-word tercets. I am deeply indebted to Jack Collom, who invented (and introduced me to) the lune form. — *JDB*

Photo by Cori Storb

www.ingramcontent.com/pod-product-compliance
Lightning Source LLC
Chambersburg PA
CBHW031202020426
42333CB00013B/775